SIGN LANGUAGE FOR PRESCHOOL

Children's Reading & Writing Education Books

All Rights reserved. No part of this book may be reproduced or used in any way or form or by any means whether electronic or mechanical, this means that you cannot record or photocopy any material ideas or tips that are provided in this book

Copyright 2016

A is for ANT

C is for CUP

D is for DESK

E is for EGG

F is for FISH

G is for GOAT

I is for INK

J is for JAR

K is for KITE

L is for LEMON

M is for MASK

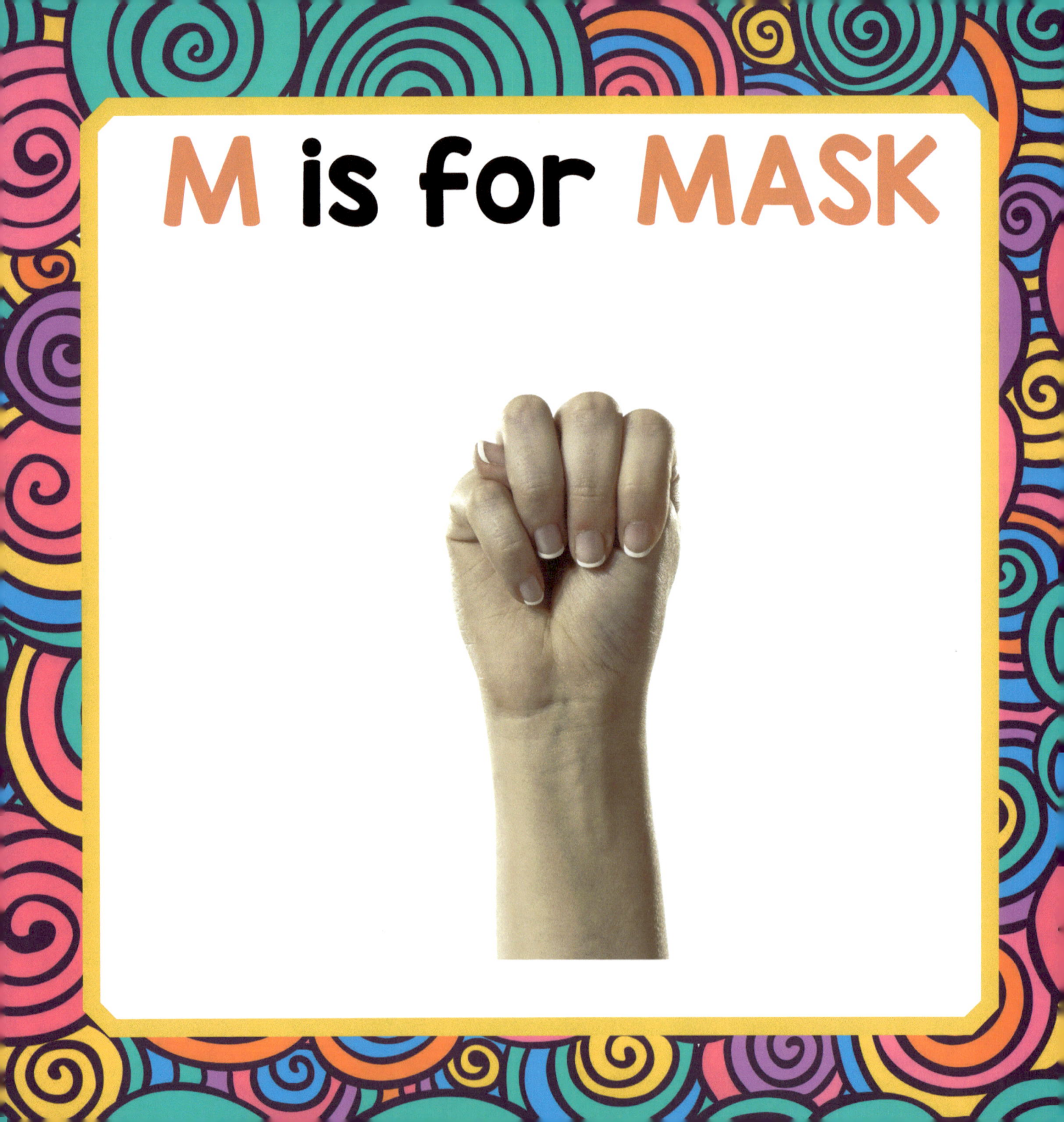

N is for NAIL

P is for PEAR

Q is for QUEEN

R is for RING

S is for SUN

T is for TREE

U is for UP

V is for VAN

W is for

X is for X-RAY

Y is for YARN

Color Hand Sign Language

Spell the following words using your hand.

Box	fun
Can	New
Duck	Mom
Sock	Dad
Pet	Top

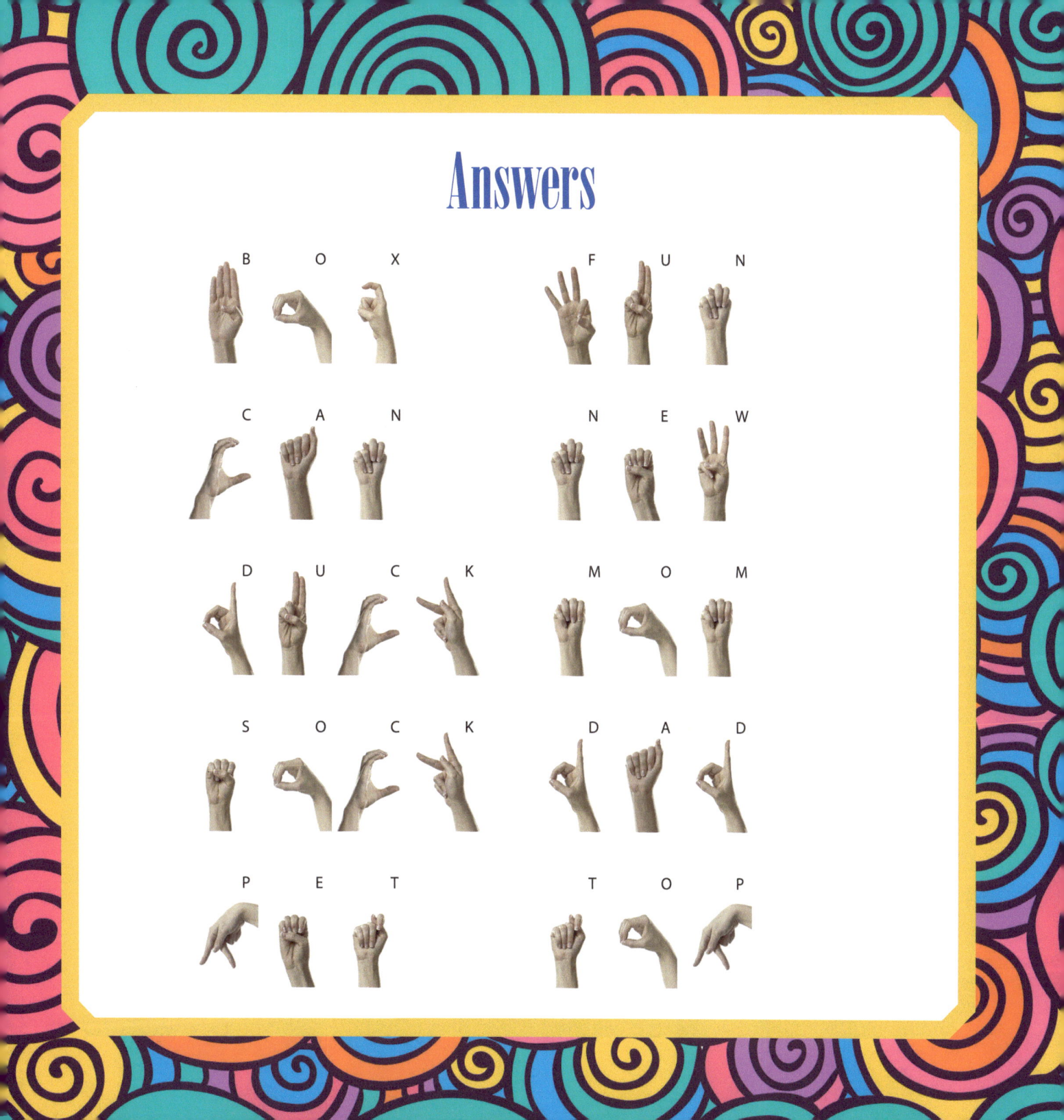

www.ingramcontent.com/pod-product-compliance
Lightning Source LLC
Chambersburg PA
CBHW041225040426
42444CB00002B/56